50

WAYS YOU CAN

SHARE

YOUR FAITH

Tony Campolo
& Gordon Aeschliman

INTERVARSITY PRESS
DOWNERS GROVE, ILLINOIS 60515

InterVarsity Press is the book-publishing division of InterVarsity Christian Fellowship, a student movement active on campus at hundreds of universities, colleges and schools of nursing in the United States of America, and a member movement of the International Fellowship of Evangelical Students. For information about local and regional activities, write Public Relations Dept., InterVarsity Christian Fellowship, 6400 Schroeder Rd., P.O. Box 7895, Madison, WI 53707-7895.

All Scripture quotations, unless otherwise indicated, are taken from the HOLY BIBLE, NEW INTERNATIONAL VERSION. Copyright © 1973, 1978, 1984 International Bible Society. Used by permission of Zondervan Publishing House. All rights reserved.

Cover illustration: Paul Turnbaugh

Printed on recycled paper.

ISBN 0-8308-1393-4

Printed in the United States of America ∞

Library of Congress Cataloging-in-Publication Data

Aeschliman, Gordon D., 1957-
   50 ways you can share your faith/by Gordon Aeschliman and Tony Campolo.
     p.   cm.
   ISBN 0-8308-1393-4
   1. Evangelistic work.   2. Witness bearing (Christianity)
   I. Campolo, Anthony.   II. Title.
   BV3790.A37   1992
248'.5—dc20   92-27353
                                                             CIP

15	14	13	12	11	10	9	8	7	6	5	4	3	2	1
03	02	01	00	99	98	97	96	95	94	93	92			

A special thanks
to some of our friends
who helped with the ideas
for this book:
Paul Borthwick
Mary Fisher
Steve Hoke
Gretchen Gaebelein Hull
Paul McKaughan
Bryant Myers
Don Posterski
Ruth Goring Stewart
Bob Yawberg
and our
wants-to-remain-anonymous
friend.

Aaargh!
. . . It's the
"E" Word!

. . . .

We think evangelism has gotten a bad rap.

Yes indeed. So often it has been described to us in such obligatory, hell-fire terms that even the sincerest, "doingest" of Christians tremble at their apparent inadequacy and disobedience to God. We cannot see anything constructive in that approach.

We hope you discover this to be a wonderfully *friendly* book on evangelism. We have not written it to bludgeon anyone into action. That style does not motivate—it just kills a good number of brain cells. We believe that basic to our Christian identity is sharing our good find with other people. It's as natural as breathing. But the very idea of evangelism has been polluted with bad preaching, guilt trips and goofy schemes that almost no one feels comfortable employing—and that offend more often than they draw people to Christ.

What we offer in this book is an assortment of fifty simple suggestions for putting evangelism to work in your world. They are as different as doing an art show and going on a camping trip. We hope you'll find a few in these pages that attract you enough that you'll be willing to experiment. Perhaps you and a few friends in your church or fellowship are adventuresome enough to risk trying them out together.

We are making a few assumptions about evangelism which we want to uncover for you before you look over our ideas.

1. We must live in the world.
We think the church has accidentally removed us from the world by calling for an unnecessary separation from those who don't find value in the church or the Christian life. Many of us have withdrawn under the guise of remaining pure or undefiled, but actually, we have simply cut the public off from Jesus.

We think that most of our lives should be lived in the "public square," that place where most of the world's people live out their daily routines. Churches that encourage otherwise are selling us personal security at the expense of the call to evangelism.

Living "in the world" can also free us from unnatural evangelistic gimmicks. The closer we are to people, the more we treat them as such. Gimmicks—those prefab gospel presentations and questionnaires—are the offerings of evangelizers who live at a safe distance from those they claim to want to reach.

2. We must learn from the world.
Most of us hold opinions regarding "the sinner" or "the un-

churched" that have very little to do with the facts. We've been told by our leaders or friends what "the others" or "they" are like, and so we carry unfair mental pictures of people who have not chosen to follow Jesus. We so easily assume they know nothing of good parenting, personal management, morality, compassion or politics. In fact, we live inside a shell that allows us no contact with them. As a result, we are never challenged to abandon our own racial, sexual, political and social prejudices.

The truth is, we have a good amount to learn from people who do not profess faith in Jesus. We need to go to them in humility and with a sincere desire to grow in our knowledge of life. All truth is God's truth. We will often discover through these relationships of mutual respect that we have been carrying around a truncated version of God's salvation plan. And we will also find that some of the people around us are much closer to the kingdom than we had realized.

3. Evangelism is God's duty.

God in his love created us, and God in his love is now pursuing us. The cross of Calvary is really just the tip of the iceberg when we look at the entire love story of God in pursuit of us. We take both *encouragement* and *hope* from the fact that evangelism is God's duty.

We find *encouragement* because we know how imperfect our love is for others. To be honest, we'd enjoy a break from this responsibility, so that we could get on with a few other personal projects. Yet God is restless with love and will not cease in wooing the people of earth until the end of time. We can rest assured that evangelism is in good hands.

We derive *hope* from this fact for ourselves—it's possible for us to become involved in evangelism and be fruitful in it, because we are in fact cooperating with the great work of God which goes on with or without us. The choice, the privilege, is ours. The highest form of human evangelism is those deeds done apart from duress, deeds that flow from a heart genuinely grateful to God for relationship with him, genuinely excited at the opportunity to peek in on the work of the Holy Spirit. This, we think, is good news and relief for the idealist.

Mellow out! Take a break! God is pleased to work with you as a partner, and while you're taking a snooze or reading for pleasure, he still works in the world and takes delight in your heart.

4. We are the aroma of Christ.

Whether or not we *intend* to give the world a whiff of Jesus, we do. This is mostly good news. Our daily life of living in the Spirit accomplishes much more for the kingdom than we imagine.

We are always surprised to hear from friends or acquaintances that they really appreciate our patience with them over relationship difficulties, our quiet and gentle endurance of pain, our tender marriages and loving manner with our children. We cannot underestimate what a powerful witness our daily walk really is.

We believe it's healthy to think more boldly of this daily living as the very heart of our evangelistic call. By our natural deeds we are painting a picture of the character of God. We're providing a backdrop that gives definition to the nature of the kingdom and the community of faith.

The bad news, of course, is that our fragrance can sometimes turn into a repugnant stench. That power wielding, those injustices, prejudices, prideful struts and outbursts of temper which we display communicate all too forcefully an aroma of self that may be mistaken for Christ's.

Perhaps what we are saying here is that all of us are called, by our life in the Spirit, to do the work of an evangelist. We do not have to shrink under the imposing shadows of the Billy Grahams. They have a special gift and calling expressed in particular ways—just as we have other gifts. All of us, though, are living testimonies of the evangel.

The approach we've chosen in this book is to help you get deeper into the world. Don't look for too many traditional expressions of evangelism. We sincerely hope that this collection of ideas will be of value to you as you live out your Christianity for the public benefit.

I

Bridge Building

· · · · · · · · · · · · · · · · ·

Here are 24 practical ideas for moving away from the Christian ghetto and into the world. Our ideas are all tried and tested. With a little bit of adjustment on your part to fit the environment you live in, we believe you'll have a lot of fun experimenting with ways to "bridge" to the world.

Quite obviously, there are far too many ideas here for one person, church or fellowship to implement. We suggest that you read through the entire batch and then carefully select five or six that could work well with your gifts and situation. We cannot emphasize enough the need to be gentle with yourself as you try out these ideas. Cry a little, laugh a lot.

1
Family Seminar
. . . .

It is just plain tough to be a parent in the United States. We don't have the advantage of some societies where life is essentially organized around the family unit; in America, parenting is battered from several sides. We need all the help we can get to build a healthy, nurturing environment where marriages, parents and children can thrive.

The family is God's creation. So much of our language regarding the faith revolves around this image: Father, Son, brother, sister, family of Christ, children of God. Our human families not only are a gift from God but also give us a glimpse at God's intentions for those who have come to a personal knowledge of Jesus. The notions of acceptance, forgiveness, security, love and community are central to our faith. And, in fact, these notions are central to the desires of all people created by God.

We suggest that churches sponsor seminars that will help us to thrive as families in today's society. How these seminars are conducted, of course, will be critical to their success both as a practical help to people in need and as a bridge to evangelism. Begin by gathering together people in your church or fellowship who feel a special call to care for families. This idea will require a good amount of time, so it's important to find coworkers who are highly motivated.

As a group, start with a curiosity to understand the particular family needs of the people who live around the church. Some church groups have put together surveys and then walked door to door in the neighborhoods, asking people what kinds of issues they wish could be covered in a seminar. You'll be surprised to find the variety of needs—from understanding the teenage years to sex education, drug intervention, lack of communication between spouses, single parenting, divorce recovery, remarriage and dealing with the empty nest.

Tabulate your responses, and then pray over the list. These are real people who have been vulnerable with you. Ask God to give you a special concern for these neighbors.

Next, look for the team of experts who can put together the content. Remember that it doesn't matter if no one from your fellowship is actually doing the teaching. What matters is that you have heard people's needs and now you are going to provide the best possible help. If you live near a Bible school, Christian college or seminary, you have the luxury of many well-trained Christians who would probably be delighted to partner with you. Show them your results, and then plan the program.

We suggest that you start small enough to make sure you manage the task well. Half a Saturday, or that plus Friday night, would be the most you could expect people to attend.

Create a readable brochure with a simple response form, and then go back to the people you initially surveyed. Tell them that you listened to their wishes and that they are welcome to attend the seminar. Put an ad in the local newspaper and, of course, rally church members around the idea so that they will invite their friends.

Make the event both helpful and enjoyable. Good music, snacks, door prizes and special resources for sale (at cost) are all musts. Ask everyone who attends to fill out an evaluation form at the end to help you determine whether or not you were on the mark. They will appreciate your sincere desire to serve them well.

You may discover that this task is too big for your fellowship. If so, look for other churches or fellowships with whom you can link up for the seminar.

One final caution: don't belittle the service to the participants by forcing evangelistic content into the seminars. Your Christian witness at this point is that you care about them enough to provide a first-rate program as a service. That message will not be lost on them, and you'll soon realize that your seminar has met a real need while pointing them to Jesus. They'll probably be back.

2

Personal Finances Seminar

· · · · · · · · · · · · ·

Some people's financial stress is almost too stagger-ing to believe. A church in Los Angeles offers seminars to its own members on managing their money. One seminar is offered exclusively to people who have trouble keeping a lid on the use of plastic money. During one of the recent seminars, the average amount owed on credit cards was $50,000.

These church members were clearly in crisis! The help offered them was so practical that the leaders decided to branch out to the general, non-churchgoing public to offer the same assistance. The response to the idea was overwhelming.

We suggest you offer the same ministry to your community.

Begin by putting together a group of motivated people who want to commit themselves to this form of bridge building. It may be natural to start with CPAs or successful businesspeople. Ask questions of your church or fellowship members to find out where the money squeeze is most acutely felt. Their financial needs are likely to be very close to those of non-Christians.

Once you have established a pretty good profile on church members' financial needs, take to the streets to find out whether those needs match your neighborhood's needs. Explain that you want to sponsor a financial workshop to provide practical help to community members. Not only will this ensure that your seminar is "on the money," but you will have also done a little advance promotion. The financial needs are going to range from buying or refinancing a home to planning an estate, sheltering money for kids' education, putting together a quality résumé, managing debt, budgeting and declaring bankruptcy (one out of every 120 American families is currently in bankruptcy).

Now that you have all the data in hand, get the team back together to plan the seminars. It may be a good idea to start with just one of the needs if the task seems overwhelming. Don't depend on your own level of understanding to meet these needs. Go to the experts for advice, and solicit their partnership in conducting the seminars.

You may even discover that your local professional societies would be willing to volunteer their help—especially if you are offering the seminar as a no-cost service to the community (the professionals will receive the benefit of exposure to potential clients).

Announce the event as widely as your church normally reaches. Pay attention to little details, such as music, snacks and additional resources for purchase. Work at putting people at ease. Remember not to "set them up" for a gospel presentation. The fact that you as a church or fellowship are responding directly to the real needs of your community is witness enough. These people will respect the integrity of a well-done seminar that did not turn out to be a sophisticated form of entrapment—something they probably expected but were willing to go through for the benefit of the practical help. Ask them to evaluate the helpfulness of the seminar, once it is over, and begin plans to broaden your financial services.

3
Polaroid
Photos

· · · · · · · · · · ·

An average-size church recently asked the question,
"What can we offer as a fun, totally free, and unexpected service
to our community to illustrate that the gospel comes free of
charge?"

A creative team put together a very simple and wonderfully
successful idea. During the warm months they visited community parks. There families of all sorts were enjoying each other—
playing baseball and soccer, doing the BBQ thing, reading, stroll-
ing with the baby, opening birthday gifts. . . . Armed with a
Polaroid camera, the church members approached the different

groups and offered to take free pictures of the family events so that the participants could hold on to the memory. No one turned down the offer.

Once the photo was developed (a whole sixty seconds), the team members put a little sticker on the back with the simple message that it was their pleasure to offer the free service. The church's address and phone number were included. No speeches or any suggestion that now you owe our church a visit. Just a quiet, delightful enrichment of somebody's day. The world could handle a few more of these types of encounters.

Another reason we really like this idea is that anyone can do it. No special training seminars are required, no bulky workbooks or memorized outlines. Rather than spending a big chunk of your free time learning how to make contact with people, you can simply get out of the TV chair and go to it. It's fun for friends to do together and a surprisingly simple way to involve junior-high or high-school youth.

You may want to enlarge on the concept a little. Offer to do a free photo shoot or videotaping of certain milestone events: twenty-fifth wedding anniversary, first baby, retirement day or family reunion. If your church has a few professional photographers, you may even consider offering an annual photo opportunity to non-churchgoing neighbors. You could do the photo shoot for free and offer them an honest at-cost price for reprints.

People will always remember that you were willing to take the time to record days that were special to them. Who else is taking the trouble to care for strangers?

4
Car Wash

· · · · · · · · · · · ·

People do not really *need* a clean car. But most of us like a clean car, and few of us enjoy doing the cleaning.

A small country church in the Northwest decided that dirty cars made for a wonderful evangelism opportunity. Their little town of 3500 has only three grocery stores. Most of the town's cars show up at one of these three parking lots at least once a week.

Every day after school for a week, the church's youth group divided into three groups and went after cars in the parking lots. The assignment was simple enough: put a little slip under the windshield wipers. The message read, "We are the high school youth of XYZ church. This Saturday we want to wipe the dirt out of our town. Your car is invited to a free and superb wash job at ABC gas station." The gas station chosen for the wash sits next door to the largest of the grocery stores. Patrons could leave their cars off to be cleaned while they did their shopping.

The turnout, as you would guess, was tremendous.

And there were no nasty surprises—you know, tracts stuffed into glove boxes, under seats, inside air-conditioning vents and the spare-tire hub. No, all that was offered was a respectful, free service.

A key element of this event was that the youth did a bang-up job of cleaning. They vacuumed floors and trunks, scrubbed wheels and fenders and washed the windows squeaky clean. In order to avoid the sense that people were obligated to pay, a poster at the entrance said, "We really are doing this for free. If you want to put a tip in the box under this poster, we'll gladly accept it. All funds will go directly to the community fund for single moms."

This evangelistic bridge is particularly good for involving high schoolers and college students. They have lots of energy, love a group effort that is rowdy and immediately rewarding, and find that this is a nonthreatening way to become involved in outreach.

If your group is energetic enough, you may even be able to offer this as a regular community service once a month during the warmer part of the year. A good number of church members would need to cooperate with this effort.

It would be natural for church members themselves to freeload on this available service. Why not take advantage of this tendency? Remind the church members that this is a *community* outreach. If they themselves want a clean car, ask them to use the car wash but pay the "church rate" of $5.00. This will subsidize the pizza blowout at the end of the day.

5
Recreation Room

· · · · · · · · · · ·

Peer pressure is like gravity: you can't ignore it or pre-tend it doesn't exist. In fact, to do so can be fatal—like stepping off the roof of a ten-story building.

We manage our lives around the fact of gravity. That doesn't mean that gravity controls us; rather, it means that we respect its power and therefore avoid foolish behavior.

Youth, especially junior high and high schoolers, are victimized by peer pressure until they are given the tools to manage their lives around this incredible force. So often they are drawn into choices and lifestyles that are immediately detrimental to themselves (for example, drug abuse) and choices that draw them further and further away from the possibility of living under the influence of the gospel. Evangelistic organizations claim that the majority of decisions made by North Americans to follow Jesus are made by the age of eighteen.

We have an idea that assists youth in their struggle with peer pressure while providing a bridge to Jesus. We suggest that churches and fellowships band together to establish youth centers near schools. The idea could be implemented on a tiny scale or a grand one. If only a few young folks are helped, the reward is beyond price.

At minimum, we would suggest renting a storefront. It could be staffed through a rotating schedule of several cooperating youth workers during the after-school hours. The location should be given a youthful, contemporary name and provide an environment where youth feel safe and at home. The atmosphere should reflect their culture. Murals, posters, contemporary music, vending machines, pinball machines, video games and pool are a few items that would create a natural environment. It would make sense to operate a small kitchen with free coffee and juice, and even to offer a sandwich menu at a reasonable price.

Christian youth publications such as *Campus Life* and *Contemporary Christian Music* would help make the case that it's not necessary to throw away one's youth culture to become a Christian. In this way a bridge to their culture is established. Churches or fellowships could easily expand the hours to evenings and weekends to offer an alternative to the destructive choices young people face.

The youth center, as its reputation grows, could become the

site for evangelistic Bible studies. Because the location would not carry the same stigma that a church building may, Christian kids could feel comfortable inviting their friends to spend one evening a week exploring the claims and life of Jesus. Not only would high-school Christians be given a viable bridge for evangelism, but they would be encouraged that their love for Jesus is not a shameful fact that has to be hidden away from peers.

6
Gift Wrapping
· · · · · · · · · · · ·

Here is an idea that can work once a year—at Christ-mas. If you live in a city with malls, you know the frantic, almost hostile, mood that surrounds last-minute buying for the loved ones (or is it the must-buy-for-them ones?). Along with the clanging of the Salvation Army bell and the blaring of carols, children are being scolded, babies are crying from neglect, spouses are arguing on budget choices and newlywed couples are going through depression at having to say no to the larger portion of their wish list. How about interrupting this seasonal "downer" with a smile and a special service?

We suggest that you offer a free gift-wrapping service. Most malls allow seasonal businesses to set up shop in the walkways. The rental and materials cost could easily be carried by a fellowship, or group of fellowships, motivated to this form of outreach.

We recommend that you involve everyone in your fellowship to secure the supplies. It would be easy enough if everyone provided a few rolls of wrapping paper, a roll of tape and ribbons. A very warm touch would be a little treat of homemade cookies for each person served. Included with the cookie could be a little note saying that the gift wrapping is done compliments of XYZ church. Phone number and address too, of course.

One church that is already offering this Christmas service reports that not only are people visiting their church because of the little note but often, while waiting for their gifts to be wrapped, people ask who is behind the effort. A simple answer regularly leads to conversations about personal needs and hardships. Prayer and counseling follow naturally. For some reason, the emotions linked to the season often prompt people to articulate their needs in ways they may not usually feel free to do.

This service is a great bridge to evangelism and a perfect form of involvement for retired people or nonworking adults whose children are grown or in school. The perfect characteristics for your potential worker are a cheerful spirit, a good listening ear, a serving attitude and a sensitivity to need that borders on intuitive.

7

Red Carpet

· · · · · · · · · · · ·

Nothing can be quite so lonely as moving to a new neighborhood. For children and adults alike, the event is often traumatic.

Think for a moment of all the changes:
- [ ] lost friends
- [ ] lost scenery
- [ ] new services
- [ ] new schools
- [ ] different recreation
- [ ] different restaurants
- [ ] different transportation

This list is far from complete. Actually, moving is considered one of the most stressful experiences we can undergo.

We suggest that you actively search out the new people in your neighborhood and think through all the ways you can help them adjust and feel at home. Start off with a warm welcome, including some move-in treats (fruit basket or cookies), and then offer to orient them to life in the new town. If they are interested in your offer, ask them some questions about their family, vocation, former home and hobbies. Share these details with friends back at your fellowship or church to see whether there are special ways you can roll out the red carpet. Here are some practical suggestions:

☐ Try to link their kids with children of similar age and interest. For example, if their daughter had been active with Campfire Girls, try to get her connected to that same activity in the new town. Or if she was a good basketball player, find out how to introduce her to her new school basketball coach.

☐ If the family is interested in cultural affairs, introduce them to the local art, music, museum and movie world. Let them know of the special annual cultural events and, if you are located near a university, get them on the arts mailing list.

☐ Be practical to the point of explaining transportation systems, good repair stores, laundry facilities, police, fire and social service centers, bargain stores and gardening seasons.

☐ If someone from your fellowship originally came from the same region as the newcomers, get them together. Sometimes we downplay the amount of culture shock one has to go through when relocating even within the United States.

The list of possibilities is endless. We suggest that your fellowship identify who would like to be a part of this kind of bridge building. Make sure that the group includes at least a couple of people who have moved across the state line. Put up a flip chart, and think through all the adjustments that may be a part of relocating. Apply these ideas when reaching out to the new neighbors, and watch how practical service like this reflects Jesus' words "I was a stranger, and you took me in."

8
Reading Room

· · · · · · · · · · · ·

Some people are unable to give their lives to Jesus simply because they have had no credible intellectual encounter with Christians. Unfortunately, some religious groups have belittled the mind in matters of faith, to the point of suggesting that we have to put away our intellect if we are to take childlike steps toward Jesus.

This kind of thinking does not reflect our Creator, who made the mind, nor does it reflect the biblical injunction that we are to love the Lord *with all our mind.* Intellectual questions regarding Christianity should always be received as sincere inquiries

by people who are seeking relationship with the One who created them. We should not ignore the questions, nor should we
imply that because we have placed our faith in Jesus, we auto-
matically have those issues personally resolved.

The college years become the dividing line for many people.
In the academic setting, young people often encounter disturb-
ing questions regarding the conflict between empirical thinking
and spiritual insights. Christianity is often pictured as a super-
stitious hangover from the Middle Ages—and the church as a
collection of simple souls who are blissfully unaware that the
sciences have all but nullified their prized dogma. Courses on
literary criticism and philosophy may bring up troubling contra-
dictions in biblical thought without offering adequate explana-
tions of how those issues might be resolved.

On the one hand we could say it is unfair that Christianity
is not properly represented in these institutions. On the other
hand, we Christians need to accept responsibility for showing
the world that we can be Christians while keeping our minds
intact! Too often we haven't listened carefully to the criticisms
aimed at our faith. Rather, we've become defensive and labeled
the "agitators" as Christian-bashers and instruments of Satan.

Sincere questions regarding the mind and faith present an
opportunity for witness. The defensive posture is not an appropriate response.

We recommend that fellowships or churches get together to
sponsor campus reading rooms (near campus, if you cannot get
on the premises). Begin by identifying people in the university
town or district who have developed a good reputation for articulating the intellectual basis of the faith in the face of con-

temporary questions. You may find these people among the faculty or in Christian campus organizations.

Pray together for a deep love of people who struggle intellectually with Christianity. Remember, the goal of this reading room is not to pin the opponent's mind to the mat, but rather to establish a sincere and honest bridge to this person's quest for truth.

Once your group senses a unified vision and love for the university community, make up a list of the resources that can best help you build the bridge. Then create an environment that is "mellow" and conducive to reading, discussion and reflection. Build bookcases to hold the classic philosophical pieces that challenge the Christian faith, and include with them the classic rebuttals to those questions.

Have a contemporary shelf that offers the latest in critical Christian thinking. Stock newspapers and magazines that help establish Christianity as a credible contemporary voice in the arena of intellectual debate.

Pay attention to other details, such as good classical music or jazz for background music. Offer ten-cent coffee and tea. Staff the reading room with people who have a personal commitment to building bridges of love to those who are asking the questions. The hours during which you keep the room open will simply reflect the availability of volunteer staff.

Funding the room is easy enough. Ask local churches and fellowships to sponsor magazine and journal subscriptions and a few book purchases. Set up the reading room as a bookstore with major Christian publishers, and order the best books from them at wholesale prices. Sell those books to the public at just enough of a markup to subsidize incidental costs.

It's our conviction that Christianity does stand up to the questions of the day. We need not fear those who raise the questions—we should encourage them to try the water that quenches thirst forever.

9
New Mothers

· · · · · · · · · · · · ·

The shock of bringing your first child into the world is more than anyone can really describe in advance. The miracle of it is a mystery that clings to the parent for days, like a warm spring aroma. The physical drain is the other shock. An infant's demands are immediate and nonstop.

Some new mothers have the good fortune to be surrounded by family or friends who are able to devote many hours of supportive care. What about those not so fortunate? A medium-sized New England church came up with a creative idea. Why not offer a free meals-and-housecleaning service to new, exhausted moms? The idea was easy enough to implement. This is what they did.

An announcement was made for interested church members to attend a planning/strategy session. Their ideas were gathered on a flip chart. Before long, a good list of simple menus was assembled and a plan of attack was implemented. Church members volunteered to be on cooking duty.

When a new mom-in-need was identified, the "cook line" was activated (not unlike a prayer line), and cooks brought their meals to the church office on designated evenings. The meals were quickly delivered to the mom. The goal was to get one to two full weeks of dinners to the home. Because the committee came up with the menus in advance, church members were not under pressure to coordinate with other cooks; the task was made simple.

Next in planning was to secure the youth group's help. The decision was made to attempt two cleaning sweeps of the new mom's home. The youth were divided into groups of three and given basic training in housecleaning. They were linked up with supervisors—retired women and men who wanted to get in on the action. Mothers were offered this service once they received the first few meals, and none of them turned the offer down. The youth were able to work quickly and efficiently with their supervisors, taking no more than a couple of hours to do a complete job.

The key was to identify mothers in need. Church members who had neighbors were one chief source of names, and the local social services office was the other. At no point did the Christians imply that church attendance ought to follow as reciprocation for their kindness. They just offered a cheery, warm and expert service to people who were experiencing a special need. And you can be sure that their witness was not missed.

10
Work Projects

· · · · · · · · · · · ·

There is a lot of talk that youth are "just not as respon-
sible as they used to be." A good number of local ills are blamed
on young people who are undisciplined, rebellious and unable
to properly twist the lid back onto the ketchup bottle. Those
complaints may be true of some teenage types, but not all.

Our suggestion is to involve your church youth group in easy,
helpful neighborhood tasks that will both truly benefit the residents and stir up curiosity about youth who are so unlike the
stereotype.

Pick out a block near the church, and have the youth group

go door to door with a simple survey, explaining that on a given Saturday they will be showing up en masse to volunteer for any yard or household task that can use five or six youth for a full hour. Articulate clearly that it is a free, no-strings-attached offer from the feisty, friendly youth of BCD church.

The goal during the survey is to get five or so projects that can be polished off in the better part of a Saturday morning and afternoon. Be sure to have your survey include questions about equipment requirements: should we bring our own lawn mowers, rakes, paint brushes and so on?

Do this once a month during the warmer part of the year. Some fellowships may want to saturate a block—that is, keep going back to the same one each month. Others may pick a different block each month for the year and then repeat the whole cycle next year. All told, your youth will have worked for twelve days that year; they will have experienced a positive means of establishing bridges for the gospel; their parents will be thrilled beyond words at the acquisition of good work habits that no doubt will transfer to home; and the youth pastor will likely get the yes vote for a contract renewal at the annual church meeting.

Most important, though, will be a neighborhood that has experienced the gracious, nutty habit that Christians have of doing good to others. Curiosity will be piqued, and some folks will no doubt insist on tipping well enough to allow some major pizza scarfing at the end of the workday.

11
Mercy Corps

· · · · · · · · · · · ·

Calamities are never welcomed into our lives, but un-fortunately they are a part of living on this side of Eden. Heart attacks, car accidents, suicides, job losses or evictions are too often visited upon those we know, and we feel paralyzed to respond to their tragedy.

In such times the gospel needs to be presented in a silent, tender, practical way, for mere words may offer no more help than an irritating, clanging bell. Job experienced that phenomenon.

We have an idea that would involve two levels of commitment

from the church. The first level would simply be an alert membership that is willing to take the time to inquire specifically about people's needs. There are several ways to do this.

Have you ever driven past a car accident and wondered how the people fared, but didn't know how to involve yourself? We suggest that whenever it's safe to pull off the road at the scene of an accident, you do so. Identify yourself as part of the volunteer clergy from your fellowship, and ask if there is anything you can do to help. You may discover a need for immediate transport, phone calls, hospital visitation or comfort of the bereaved. Be careful not to move victims or attempt any first aid treatment for which you are not trained.

Help all you can on the spot, and then volunteer the church's services for any further acts of mercy that are needed. The church could print up special business cards for this group of volunteers, so that accident victims have a means of contact (they may be willing to give you their phone number and address too).

The possibilities on the other side of this simple pull-over are endless. The volunteer mercy corps is the second group required. Their job is to go the next mile.

Make contact with the family if they allowed a follow-up phone number. Find out several ways to become involved in their need. This could be as simple as cooking a couple of meals or as difficult as sitting with those who have lost a loved one, making hospital visits to victims of drunk drivers or providing transport to physical therapy sessions.

The mercy corps need not limit itself to road accidents. Assume a posture of listening for human need. Read the local paper, listen to the talk at local coffee shops, inquire among neighbors and ask at the local social welfare office. Some towns have a chaplain who works inside the police force—another gold mine of information about human need.

The bottom line is this: the church is at its best when it serves both as a listening post for society's pain and as a compassionate minister to those hurts. Nothing more accurately and precisely illustrates the gospel than this type of community in action. And nothing is as effective in establishing a bridge to evangelism.

We admit it: this idea will be the most time-consuming of all our suggestions, but it is the heart of the evangelistic work of the church. Anyone can be a part. This outreach is simply the integrity of the gospel being lived out, illustrating the words of Jesus to John's disciples in Matthew 11:5: "The blind receive sight, the lame walk, those who have leprosy are cured, the deaf hear, the dead are raised, and the good news is preached to the poor."

12
Chaplaincy
············

It is possible that your church or fellowship has a member who is qualified to fit your city's profile of a volunteer chaplain. Hundreds of sheriff's departments in the United States understand the value of a pastoral presence to help manage the pain of human tragedy. This is not a question of church encroaching on state, but rather a sensible agreement between church and state that we are emotional, spiritual beings and thus need special care during hardships.

The value of this volunteer program is that a chaplain is on call twenty-four hours a day for the most extreme cases of need. Usually the chaplain is called in for help if there has been a death or some other traumatic event. The chaplains are given the freedom to provide whatever comfort is appropriate and will often be involved with follow-up visits to the home, hospital or jail. Because they are in touch with both the need and the Christian community, they are able to mobilize resources to meet specific needs.

If there is no chaplaincy program in your town, ask the sheriff's department how you might get one started. Find out what they are able to contribute and what requirements they have for the chaplaincy. In many cases, sheriff's departments will outfit the volunteer with a uniform, a vehicle (equipped with radio and emergency lights) and a training seminar sponsored by the state. The chaplain typically works under the supervision of the sheriff (though not as an employee) and is expected to be ordained by a recognized denomination.

You as a church or coalition of churches would be expected to provide the salary of the chaplain if this person needs to make a living. In this case, a local fund is opened at a bank for local businesses and churches to deposit gifts toward the chaplain's salary. Most often, the sheriff's department will ask that a local committee be formed to manage the financial end, because of the potential conflict between church and state.

Many churches have been able to coordinate with other fellowships to assemble a pool of chaplains—mostly retired pastors and missionaries. This is an appropriate recognition of the giftings of people who may have been shoved into inactivity for no other reason than that they have reached a certain age. They may be very skilled for this work and may need little or no remuneration.

13
Think Tank

· · · · · · · · · · · · · ·

Ever found yourself in a bind and wished there was just one person who could offer you good, practical advice about handling the crisis? It's not true that if we were just smart enough we'd be able to answer all our own questions. We live in a highly technological, specialized, detailed society, with rules and pitfalls to fill volumes in the local library. There is rarely a simple, obvious answer to modern dilemmas.

Our idea here, however, is simple. We think the church can turn life's complex and baffling situations into an opportunity for service and a bridge to the family of Christ. Most fellowships include some professionals: real estate agents, bankers, CPAs, tax experts, vocational counselors, social workers and the like. We propose that your fellowship offer a weekly get-together for people who want to bring their questions and dilemmas to a public forum.

The church can set up a little committee of "pros" who show up each time and interact with the community members. The process does not have to be threatening or require participants to be vulnerable. Encourage people to take an approach like this: "My uncle Ernest has been told by the city council that it is his responsibility to put in a new curb in front of his house. The price tag is $12,000. The city will lend him the money at five per cent interest. When my uncle bought the house, he had no idea that this would be a city requirement. What can he do?" (This is a real story, by the way.)

Community members can all pitch in with advice and wisdom from experience (and outrage!), and probably some of the professionals will have solid counsel to solve the dilemma. The word will get out after a while that IJK church offers a great service for helping folks manage life's complexities.

Do make it clear that this is not a sales opportunity—that is, the professionals are not volunteering their time so as to get your business later. This needs to be another one of those absolutely free services inexplicably offered by a local church. People should leave ready to tell their friends, "They didn't pressure me to give anything in return; they seemed to be genuinely interested in my welfare!"

What a wonderful bridge to Jesus.

14
24-Hour
Help Line
●●●●●●●●●●●

A woman in her thirties who lives in the Midwest tells the story of how she got started in a ministry to her neighborhood:

"I had always been a healthy, energetic person. The car accident that resulted in the loss of my two legs was a deep emotional blow. My mobility was gone, I could no longer play my favorite sports and, hard as I tried, I was unable to find employment. Eventually, I became so depressed I just moped about my apartment wishing the accident had killed me.

"I'm not sure what prompted the idea, but one night I suddenly got hit with the idea of praying for people. *Now there's something I can do,* I thought to myself. The idea was not particularly profound, but I put an ad in a local paper saying that I was disabled and would love to pray for anyone with special needs. I published my phone number, and the phone hasn't quit ringing since."

People long for the attention of praying saints. None of us has life completely in order, and many of us need to share our burdens with someone who is confident enough during the time of suffering to approach God for help. Unfortunately, too many people live at an emotional distance from the church. They are not sure how to approach the stained-glass building and collared minister.

We suggest that you call a special meeting for people who want to volunteer for this ministry. Pray together that God will give you a gentle, honed sensitivity to those who call in. One of the wonderful aspects of this ministry is that it can involve anyone who has a wise spirit and a love for prayer. Those who are less mobile or unable to take a regular job should receive preferential treatment in this bridge-building ministry.

Getting a hotline is easy. The miracles of modern technology allow for several volunteers to work on one line. We recommend that you rent a phone line. With a simple "call forwarding" arrangement, the calls can be forwarded to the home of whoever is on call—even outside the originating area code. Pray with the person right there on the phone, and assure him or her you will continue to pray throughout that week. Arrange a rotation schedule that covers the phone all twenty-four hours of the day.

Promote this service with an advertisement in the local yellow pages and newspaper. Be very clear that what you are offering is prayer—free of charge. No one will come after the callers for a personal visit, donation or sermon, and they won't be put on a mailing list or be expected to go to church. You can always have a little tag line that advertises this as "a free service from your friends at the EFG church."

Get the volunteers together once a week to pray corporately for the needs of those who called in. This extends your ministry beyond that initial encounter and may even open up the possibility of offshoot ministries. And it is very likely that some of the people who listened to your selfless prayers over the phone lines will visit the church for a personal encounter with people who are willing to take the time to care.

15
Camping
· · · · · · · · · · ·

Here's an idea for the brave! Or the partly crazy . . .

How about organizing a first-rate camping trip for youth? Many of us will recall how important camps were for us at certain stages of our Christian commitment. Those weeks of intensified fun and Bible study served to boost our resolve to follow Jesus and to try once again not to fall back after leaving the mountaintop experience.

We really should not belittle the value of those times. In one sense they provide an extended quiet time (youth style), and in fact, they are not very different from the currently popular spiritual retreats for adults who need to escape the hubbub of life long enough to listen to the voice of God.

Some of us made our initial decision to follow Christ at a youth camp.

Our suggestion is that you pull together the hardy campers from your church or fellowship and begin to plan. Pool your collective experience to design a real blast that is safe and age-appropriate. If no campers attend your fellowship, knock on another church's door for help, or look up your local Boy Scout/ Girl Scout troop leader.

Once the expert team is in place, do your community research to establish which age group would be best served, what camping style would be most enjoyed and which dates would be most convenient. This information could be gathered through a very simple door-to-door survey in whatever community you choose to serve. Another approach would be to involve your church youth. Ask them to take a simple form to their friends at school—friends who are currently not involved in any church program. This bridge to friendships already established can make for a casual, relaxed camping experience.

Be sure to get legal advice for sponsoring this type of event. Local lawyers or Scout troops are likely to have the needed information on hand. You will need to have waivers of all sorts signed.

Be sensitive to the youth who join the camping trip. You may be tempted to "hit them with the whole package" while they are a captive audience. Respect them. Make sure the trip is all that you advertised it to be, and allow them a genuine encounter with the people and claims of Christ at the same time. They will be back for more the next year, and they may even ask to be a part of your church's regular youth program.

16
Art
Room

· · · · · · · · · · ·

Students involved in campus evangelism will often dis-cover that there are certain groups of people to whom the gospel appears entirely irrelevant. For some reason, there is a barrier in the minds of these people, so that they simply write Christianity off as "not their thing."

We should not be too mystified by these barriers. Some people carry a painful history that leaves them with the feeling that God did not protect them in their vulnerable moments. In their experience God has seemed distant and uncaring. Perhaps they were hurt by religious leaders and consequently view all Christians as hypocrites. The church has a tremendously difficult and humbling work to do in building bridges toward people with this kind of pain.

There is another group on campus that experiences the rejection of the church: the artists. Christians are often trained to look at art as *bad*. It has no "eternal" value, it is too sensual and humanistic. Sadly, the artist, who may be closer to the creative character of God than most people, feels cut off from the church.

Here is our evangelistic suggestion: Christian artists who want to reach their peers with the message of Jesus should band together for regular prayer and artistic stimulation as they think about ways to build bridges. Then they can create an art room on campus. This studio can become the cutting edge of campus artistic creation.

With some help from people with design and construction skills, put together a super-modern studio that includes room for displays, lounging about, beverage service and live shows. Several possibilities are begging for implementation. Have students submit their work for exhibition. Rotate to a new artist each week, and place ads in the school paper. Show art that is diverse in both theme and medium. Sponsor live art—select a student sculptor or musician to set up shop for two weeks and work on the piece in the public view. Sponsor poetry readings.

Once a year sponsor a faculty week, giving art faculty the option of exhibiting their new work (less than twelve months old). Have a similar week for the local community. Once the reputation for the art room is established, we think it's realistic to secure funding to bring in a nationally acclaimed artist for an annual "Art Week" exhibition.

The art room then becomes a natural place for the art community to relax with that daily dose of espresso or cappuccino. And the groundwork will be laid for a credible witness to artists. The bulletin board can carry ads for evening Bible studies sponsored by the art room, and soon a safe haven will be created for those who were "on the fringes" to inquire about the person of Jesus.

17
Forum
· · · · · · · · · · ·

A group of Christians from a large Midwestern campus were praying together for a way to demonstrate to their college peers that Christianity is vitally concerned with the well-being of the globe. They had smarted under the blows of newspaper editorials that labeled Christians as having no real interest in the suffering of the world.

Prayer time led to discussions and eventually to the decision to take leadership on an issue that had surfaced as a general campus concern: world hunger. This group of Christians set out to design the most elaborate, informative and practical campus-wide program on hunger ever developed at that university. The impact went beyond their own dreams: the program put the Christian faith solidly on the side of the world's poor and led to several personal decisions to follow Christ.

This is how they did it. They drew up a list of prominent national leaders who were known for their work on behalf of the hungry. These people were all asked whether they would come to the campus for a high-profile program on global hunger. Several agreed to the idea.

Next, professors in political science, agriculture and community development were asked to host these leaders both in the classroom and at special departmental breakfasts. Local religious and community leaders were invited to join in a campus-sponsored debate on how to bring the global concern down to a local level.

Once all these leaders were lined up, the fellowship of Christian students approached the university leadership with the list of all the "main players" who were going to show up at the campus, plus the professors and administrators who had agreed to be a part of the event. These students suggested that the campus administration might want to announce the event as the First Annual Hunger Week.

The administration was smart enough to see the marketing value of this event and the benefit of good student relations. They agreed to the idea of a hunger week and called the press to make the announcement. The press, of course, wanted to interview the students who had provided the energy behind the idea.

When the whole program became public, the student body

saw not only an impressively coordinated event that had drawn in national leaders, but also a group of motivated Christians who had cared enough to put in time, energy and creativity.

The gospel message went out clearly.

18
Joining a Local Professional Group

· · · · · · · · · · · · ·

Christians have to deal with some tension over how to distribute their energy. The church, always looking for a few warm bodies to staff programs, preaches the need for us to become more involved in its functions so that it can better fulfill its evangelistic and discipleship callings. The more we answer this pastoral plea (sometimes it's more of a pastoral harangue), the more our weeknight and weekend calendar looks as if we are doubly employed—by our job and by our church.

The problem is that very few of these volunteer tasks actually take us outside the church community, or even outside the building. In effect, we spend the bulk of these volunteer hours serving ourselves. Yet we've been called to be *in the world*.

Our feeling is that pastors should encourage their members to give as much time to community projects as to church committees. If we are truly concerned that the kingdom of Christ pervade all of society, then we need to be sure that our bodies are present.

Find out which professional groups meet regularly in your own town, and decide how much time you can reasonably budget to be a part of these clusters. Pick a group that will expand your understanding of the town, that will stretch your comfort zone. If you have never visited a Rotary or Kiwanis meeting, this may be a good place to start.

Generally, these service organizations do a lot of good for the community. This being the case, it's absolutely consistent with our Christian faith to link up with their efforts. Plus, you will have the experience of working in an arena that often welcomes people who do not feel welcomed by the church.

We offer one caution: It is possible to enter these new groups with a severe case of piousness—the attitude that we're coming in with the eventual goal of "getting these heathen saved." That approach is extremely dangerous and counterproductive. Go in fully armed with a humble, teachable spirit, genuinely motivated to join with others to serve society. Remember, the good Samaritan gave first aid, not a sermon.

19
A Service Project
· · · · · · · · · · · ·

Too often we cherish the stereotype that people who don't have a personal knowledge of Christ don't care about the world's ills; they just care about themselves. Interestingly enough, others often apply that stereotype to Christians—those people who live with their heads in the clouds and have no concern for things of this world.

Here's a suggestion for rubbing shoulders with people in a new way that would correct both stereotypes and probably stir up a curiosity about Christ: Become involved in community projects that are clearly directed toward the betterment of society. We recommend linking up with projects that are not specifically or at least not blatantly "Christian."

Most cities need volunteers to help youth through Big Brother/Big Sister partnerships or recreation programs. There are projects to build homes (with Habitat for Humanity, for example) for people who would not ordinarily be able to afford one of their own, to construct temporary shelters for the homeless or to plant trees and gardens to help reverse the negative impact our lifestyle is having on the environment. And Adopt-a-Highway cleanup is spreading.

Some people may be shocked to find Christians volunteering for projects that are not church-controlled. Yet we have seen how conversations develop around a specific need and how eventually a surprised individual may feel comfortable enough to pursue the relationship further. Conversation over dinner leads easily to a discussion of why one is motivated to spend free hours on service projects. It is distinctly Christian to have these kinds of concerns. Joint service projects are one of the best ways to live out our faith in public.

One church took the idea a little further: They contacted city hall and announced that they'd like to shoulder some of the responsibility for the city's special needs. They offered a dozen youth and as many adults for a two-week stretch in the summer and said, in effect, "Put us to work."

You can imagine that the press picked up the story (unfortunately, in their view, Christians' volunteering their time was a newsworthy event!), and soon other churches wanted to get in on the action. What can the public say about a group of people who not only pay taxes to hire others to do the "dirty work" but also show up to become personally involved?

Jesus asks us to do our good works in such a way that people will be prompted to glorify the Lord in heaven. No big glitz or glory—just the quiet witness that the words we use to convey the gospel are not only valuable in themselves but are backed up with deeds.

20
Town Meeting

· · · · · · · · · · · ·

The concept of a town meeting is not foreign to Americans. It used to be the chief way of hearing citizens' complaints and the forum for discussing ideas or proposals. The town meeting is revived about every four years—curiously linked with the cycle of presidential campaigns. Although a bit suspect because of the raw nature of these gatherings (candidates want to hear what people are feeling in order to articulate positions that will win the popular vote), these town meetings have exposed the needs of the public in a way that no other meeting could.

Our idea is for the church to learn from this model and implement it as a genuine means of hearing people's needs and perspectives. This is how you might go about it: Collect a group of church or fellowship members who have a strong interest in community affairs. Discuss the issues that seem to be "hot" in your community.

It would be great if there were some way to include people who are involved professionally in city affairs (for instance, a lawyer, principal, peace officer or social worker). If you're unable to include professionals on the committee, we suggest you get some of their input through appointments—they will be flattered by the attention.

Next, you need to go directly to the community to conduct a survey. Show people the list of issues that have emerged so far, and ask how well these items reflect personal concerns. How would they see it differently? What would they add to the list? Explain the idea of the town meeting. Poll for the best times, and tell them to look for the announcement. Finally, ask them what sort of people they'd like to have present to hear their concerns.

Several goals will be achieved with this kind of research. First, you are getting the word out that the upcoming meeting will reflect real concerns. Second, you are showing that you're interested in hearing people's opinions. Third, you are giving the first session a jump-start.

Take all the findings back to the committee. Pray together that God will give you the ability to hear people clearly and that you will be able to respond compassionately and effectively. Contact city officials with your plan to hold a town meeting. Show them the issues that have emerged and the names of officials whom local residents said they would like to hear from directly.

Go over the calendar to come up with the best date for all concerned. Then get the word out. Secure the assistance of a good artist to make up a small flyer and a poster. Approach your local newspaper and radio station to see if they will give the event free promotion. Even if they won't, at least they'll have been made aware of the event, and reporters will probably show up to listen to the public and write up the issues. Then pray like crazy, and hold the first meeting.

Our recommendation is that the meeting be chaired by someone who has had plenty of experience fielding questions and opinions. Open the meeting by thanking people for showing up. Explain that the event is sponsored by HIJ church, and tell them that your main goal is to give people a chance to hear what those around them really think. Say that the church itself would like to understand the issues better in order to be more valuable to the community, and that you hope city officials will also hear the same issues loud and clear. Let them know that this evening is the first round, and therefore experimental—if people find it valuable, the church will sponsor another.

The meeting will accomplish a great deal. First, the church is hearing the people firsthand. This kind of information demands action. You have to go back and pray about how your church can be a steward of the new understanding. Let's hope the direct outcome will be a church whose ministry is much better attuned to people's needs. Second, a forum has been created for city hall. The officials will have been served notice (a good switch) regarding their performance. Because it will be a regular affair, this town meeting, if it continues, will rise above campaign politics.

Finally, community members will see a "city set on a hill." The witness of a church that cares will have gone out powerfully and clearly. This is as evangelistic as it gets, and it will keep the local fellowship hopping with outreach opportunities beyond its ability to respond.

21
Vacation Coffee House
· · · · · · · · · · · ·

Here is a seasonal evangelistic idea. One beach city in the South attracts large numbers of tourists in the summer. A local pastor saw the evangelistic possibilities and got on the phone with several other local pastors. This was the outcome of those calls.

Church members who owned property on or near the beach were asked to come to a special brainstorming session. Close to a dozen businesspeople from the different churches in town showed up, and the pastors asked these Christians to commit themselves to an evangelistic outreach. The plan was to provide an inexpensive, comfortable coffee house for tourists, where Christian literature and music would provide an environment that would encourage curious people to pursue the faith further.

The churches transformed part of an underused warehouse into a modern coffee house. Schedules for permits and remodeling were drawn up well in advance, and all the cooperating churches and businesses put money in to underwrite the operation.

By the time summer arrived, an attractive coffee shop, staffed by church volunteers, was open to the public. Foot traffic was the main source of the patrons. Two nearby hotels were targeted for flyer distribution, advertising an "inexpensive, comfortable coffee house operated by a coalition of local businesspersons and clergy." The promotion did not hide the Christian connection. Most vacationers, already over budget before their vacation was half begun, were happy for the service.

The coffee-house bulletin board announced local church services, and each table had little business cards that offered help "should you run into a little trouble while on vacation." Calls for help did come in: "We've lost our child," "We can't find our travelers' checks," "There's been an accident, and our parents are in the hospital—can you help us?" Others called wanting to talk more about the Christian faith.

The committee is now considering opening a second coffee shop for the next season.

22
Prayer Breakfast

· · · · · · · · · · · ·

The Bible instructs us to pray for those who are in authority over us. Sometimes that's pretty easy to do—for example, if we happen to agree with the political platform of the person who won the election. But God calls for something much more demanding than simply supporting a structure that gives us political security.

Many cities throughout the United States have experienced the cooperative work of Christians who believe in the value of prayer, who obey Christ's call to intercede. We suggest that every town, city, county and state should have the blessing of being prayed over. We recommend that at minimum Christians come together once each year to pray for those who are in authority at these different levels of government.

Prayer has three different functions in this regard. The first is the most important and the central function of prayer: Scripture tells us that prayer moves God. We cannot understand this mystery; it is too much for our finite minds to hold. But the privilege of prayer is there for the taking. When we bring our hearts together to pray for the welfare of our cities, to pray that God will provide special wisdom to our leaders and direct the difficult decision-making processes of government, we are actually stirring God into action.

Second, our prayer is a specific form of caring for those who are in leadership. There are times when we serve notice to those in authority regarding certain regulations, laws and practices. But that's not the agenda of a prayer breakfast. This is a time to surround the leader with our good will and support. We are saying to this person, "We want the best for you. We are pleading with the One we worship and serve to provide you with all you need to govern—and our prayers are not partisan." Elected officials need this sort of caring. No matter what their motivations are, they are fallible people and require the support of peers who respect the office they fill.

The third function of this kind of prayer is perhaps the clearest evangelistic bridge to politicians and officeholders: our statement of love and unity in a field that thrives on divisiveness, slander and malice. Thus we show that Christians can hold divergent opinions on laws and programs while still regarding others more highly than themselves. The prayer breakfast is a physical experience of the body of Christ at work.

If you decide to work for this idea in your area, begin by meeting with pastoral staff from different churches. You need to pray together regularly to allow God the opportunity to begin melding you into a unified team, each convinced of the other's heart for the leaders, the region and the nation. If you do not do this important groundwork, the prayer breakfast could easily disintegrate into a partisan religious spectacle that will increase political leaders' cynicism about the church. In your times together, pray for your leaders by name: mayor, judges, senators, supervisors and so forth.

When you believe you are ready to go public, coordinate your calendar with public officials' calendars. Announce the event as a unified Christian commitment to pray for those in authority. List the cooperating churches and the political leaders who will be present.

Besides the food and entertainment that usually accompany this type of event, make sure that the central focus is prayer for the specific, actual needs of each leader represented there. If you have been praying regularly for these leaders, they will be surprised at the ease with which you bring them before the Father. They will be appreciative even if personally they do not believe in God or in prayer. And the politicized public will be left wondering about these strange Christians.

23
Serve the Public with Prayer

· · · · · · · · · · · ·

One of the benefits of being linked to the body of
Christ is our ability to ask others to help carry our burdens
through their prayers. We probably are unaware of how much
we naturally rely on this service of love. Be it sickness, loss of
job, a housing need, depression, anxiety, vocational decision or
marriage decision (just to name a few), we have the luxury of
sharing our burden.

People outside the faith have the same need for others to
come alongside and share their heavy load, to intercede on their
behalf for God's mercy and intervention in life's affairs. Some

have never experienced anything like this at all. Many lack even minimal support from family and friends.

We suggest a very simple prayer service that is offered in two forms. The first is the prayer booth. How many times would you have wished for the special attention of one person whose only job was to listen, anonymously, to your specific need? We think churches could easily offer this service with the help of retired or nonworking members. A notice in the local newspaper could announce the days and hours the prayer booths would operate. Volunteers would sit in the specially constructed booths (in the sanctuary) during these hours, and listen with all their hearts to the requests. And then they would pray as generously as they know how. The booths would allow private discussion and prayer; the person bringing a problem for prayer would know it was not being overheard by others.

The second approach is to announce a phone-in prayer line. This could be a dedicated phone line with an answering machine that would allow people to leave personal requests. The church would have a group of volunteers who regularly gather to listen to, and then pray over, the requests. And it's not unlikely that this type of praying could lead to a broader ministry. For example, callers might request a visit to a relative in the hospital or the local jail.

We believe prayer is the primary service that any of us can offer to the world. We also believe that more people would come to us for prayer if we offered the service in a way that would fit their lifestyles and needs.

We've described two ideas. Think up your own!

24
Letter to the Editor
• • • • • • • • • • •

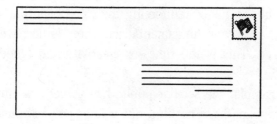

Ever wonder how you could broadcast a Christian response to local, national or international issues without paying much money? It's easy enough if you can take the time with a few friends to pen reasonable, well-thought-out letters that articulate a Christian view without being overtly evangelistic.

This is the suggestion. Link up with a small group of local Christians who have a strong interest in public issues and who know how to write. We recommend that you pray together—unifying yourselves around the purpose of evangelism—and then begin to read the letters published in local and national journals.

If you are near a large library, you won't have to spend a dime. We recommend you read letters in the *Los Angeles Times, Time, Newsweek, Greenpeace, National Review, Utne Reader, Rolling Stone* and *People*. Become familiar with the style of writing; discuss which letters you think were most effective in gaining attention and making a clear point that sticks with the reader.

Then plan. You need to ask the question: What could we say in response to local and national issues that would surprise a secular reader and stimulate curiosity about the faith? The public would naturally expect a letter from Christians decrying certain social ills, hence reinforcing the stereotype that we are a bunch of naysaying fundamentalists. There is no need to feed this image. This is the time for creativity and (good, clean) mischief.

For example, the secular public has gained the impression that Christians have nothing but a knee-jerk response to the epidemic of AIDS. There is very little Christian literature urging a compassionate response to people who are suffering with this dreadful illness. We think a thoughtful, caring Christian reflection on a current issue relating to AIDS would surprise many readers.

Similarly, too often Christians have been viewed as having very little concern for the environment: "Sure, no problem; bulldoze the forest! Jesus is coming back soon anyway!" Unfair perhaps. Perhaps not. But the stereotype is there, and we have a chance to correct it with a letter.

Look at issues on your college campus. Is there a clear case of racism or sexism? Write the editor of the campus newspaper.

The letters don't need to articulate a specific "salvation plan" or contain a lot of "Christian" language. Don't build unnecessary barriers into your writing. But do sign the letter in such a way that you identify the source—Christians Against Racism, Christian Artists Fellowship or Faith Baptist Church. Your letter may initially be read only for a laugh, but you may be the one left smiling.

II

Calendar Celebrations

· · · · · · · · · · · · · · · ·

**Our culture offers us some very natural means of "be-
ing nice" to others—Hallmark events, we might say.
Admittedly, the bottom line is business, but we don't
think that's all bad. Most people could use more affir-
mation and kind words. We are told that the chief problem children face, for example, is all the negative, ugly
images they carry in their psyche from inappropriate
scolding and name calling.**

In this section, we're simply suggesting that you take advantage of a cultural mainstay—the plethora of calendar celebrations—and look for ways to point to the person of Jesus.

25
Christmas

· · · · · · · · · · ·

We've heard enough sermons about putting Christ back into Christmas. We're not interested in adding to the guilt trip. Surely we already carry enough guilt for not being perfect in living out our Christian faith!

Christmas can be very hard on families with children. The pressure is there to provide all the goodies displayed on TV advertisements while still trying to keep Christ at the center of the season.

In the West, Christmas is basically a secular, cultural event. If there were no Christians in this part of the hemisphere, the event would still go on. We don't see the value of attacking the cultural celebration. Anyway, our nation, in our own language, has been construed as a Christian nation. Many businesses that have benefitted from the commercialization of Christmas are run by us—Christian businesspeople! We had something to do with the current status of Christmas.

Christmas is a fact. It's here to stay. Rather than going on the defensive, our suggestion is to take a positive, uplifting approach to the season. We have two ideas.

The first has to do with emotions. Counseling centers report that Christmas is their busiest time of year. All the warm, tender songs of Christmas love, the TV specials that end with happy weddings, children found and puppy dogs that got well, are only half the story. Thousands of people find Christmas to be the loneliest time of year.

Perhaps a child or spouse has died, and this Christmas will be the first without the loved one. It's too painful to join in the celebrations. All the cheer only sharpens the loss. Or perhaps the loss of a job leads to financial stress. The children end up with few presents and can't help feeling wistful when they see the glorious piles of gifts under their friends' trees. Their parents feel like failures.

We suggest that every year, a couple of months prior to Christmas, your church or fellowship assemble a committee of people who would like to direct a large part of their Christmas giving toward those who are experiencing loss. Get the word out to the rest of the fellowship that you're looking for people who are experiencing these traumas. Then organize your efforts to be specific and caring.

One church involved its youth group to buy gifts for a family whose parents were unemployed. The gifts were selected by youths of the same age as those in the distressed family—in other words, the gifts were right on target. The family didn't feel they received last-minute-rush items or "missionary barrel" castoffs.

Another congregation prayed for the families that had experienced the loss of loved ones and carefully thought through how to involve them in the season's celebrations. The ideas included going to see movies and plays with them, joining in special dinners and getting together to make crafts and decorations for homeless shelters.

Our other idea is to make gifts of volunteer labor—to be cashed in during a low point of the year. Secular institutions are usually deluged with special church programs during the Christmas season, which is great, but the rest of the year, these same organizations are often understaffed and too overloaded to put creative energy into special programs. Our suggestion is that your fellowship get together and decide how many evenings, Saturdays or weekdays it would like to give as a gift to a local hospital, hospice, convalescent home, homeless shelter, youth detention center or jail.

Make up a special coupon that announces the "gift of Christmas that keeps giving all year long." When you and your friends are volunteering in mid-April and early July, the message of Jesus will be more clearly heard than it can be in December 24th's last-minute mania.

26
Easter/Passover
· · · · · · · · · · · ·

The Easter Bunny isn't quite as popular as Santa. Per-haps that day is coming.

The mystery and splendor of Easter is almost too awesome to put into words for people who have a personal relationship with Jesus. How then do we interpret the celebration to those who are not a part of the family of faith? Do we tell them that God went to hell? That mere human beings pinned God to a piece of wood as though he were part of a moth collection? That we are no longer condemned because one person voluntarily died two thousand years ago?

Easter is the richest of Christian celebrations. Many families, recognizing this fact, have made this their annual spiritual "blowout" celebration, rather than letting Christmas take center stage.

Easter is connected to the Passover celebration that dates back yet another couple thousand years. The Israelites were close to being freed from four hundred years of Egyptian captivity. God was sending a plague throughout the land in order to convince Pharaoh to let the Israelites go free. Pharaoh was not very cooperative, so finally God announced to Moses that he was going to take the life of every first-born child in the land. The only way to escape this plague was to kill a spotless lamb and sprinkle its blood on the doorpost of one's home. This would be a sign to the angel of death to pass over that home and spare it from death on the night of the tragedy.

The image is not missed by Christians, who have been freed from the penalty of death because of their decision to place faith in the blood of Jesus which was shed on the cross of Calvary. As we celebrate the feast of the Passover Lamb, millions of Jewish people celebrate their Passover, a rich celebration filled with longing, that calls the Messiah to come and free the nation. Easter, then, presents a wonderful opportunity to learn about this Jewish holiday. It is also a tremendous bridge to Jewish friends who are curious about Jesus.

Here is our suggestion. An organization called Jews for Jesus has reconstructed the Passover feast to show how Jesus is the Messiah so desperately longed for in this Jewish celebration. Jews for Jesus has prepared a special script for those who would like to go through the celebration.

We recommend that you contact them to see if they are hosting the Passover dinner, or Seder, in your town. If not, suggest that you could get a large enough group together to make it worth their while to fly someone to your city.

Once you have experienced this celebration, consider making it an annual event. You can do it privately in your own home with Jewish friends or continue it in a public venue in cooperation with other Christian fellowships. Or go for both!

We know the folks at Jews for Jesus. They have very big hearts for Jewish evangelism and would be happy to host the meal for your town. Their address is in the Organizations section.

27
Valentine's Day

· · · · · · · · · · · ·

Who can live up to the standards of a Hollywood valen-
tine's romantic movie? That's what we thought.

But several churches have caught on to the idea of turning
this annual cards-and-roses event into a fun-filled bridge for
evangelism. Here is what they do. Church or fellowship
members who are particularly interested in encouraging the relationships of married couples get together to plan a Sweet-
hearts' Banquet. The idea is to create an evening that is especially appropriate for inviting friends who are not a part of the
faith. The possibilities are great and are limited only to the

creative gifts of your fellowship.

One church sponsored a banquet at a ritzy hotel and planned a full evening of entertainment. Because the church had a number of good musicians and theatrical professionals, the evening included first-rate live renditions of Beatles' love songs, lip syncs of the Carpenters and a dramatic, hilarious, shrunkdown version of *Romeo and Juliet*. A game show was simulated to discover which spouses knew the most about each other. Door prizes and the like made for an evening of romance and laughter.

The evening was fun and clean. No condemning words were spoken about how "the world" messes up relationships and leads us into debauchery. Rather, a firm, positive alternative was offered in an atmosphere of love and acceptance.

There were no blatant sales pitches for joining the church. The pastoral team prayed before the meal, closed the evening with prayer, and simply invited people to "peek in at the church" sometime if they were interested. "We'd sure love you to."

28
New Year's Day

Doesn't it seem to you that sometimes we Christians work really hard to be boring? While the world out there throws some pretty wild parties to bring in the new year, we force our little ones to try to stay awake through another sermon on keeping resolutions, not failing Jesus again this year or some other depressing, guilt-inflicting message that causes children to swear they'll never attend church when they grow up. And to make it worse, we close the evening with a long prayer meeting.

Now obviously, none of these elements is wrong. It's just that the fit is not right for the season. The approach is not sensitive to the alternatives being offered by society. It's as though the more remote and boring our New Year's Eve event becomes, the more self-righteous we feel.

Our suggestion is simple. Design a blowout evening that is appropriate to the age levels in your community. It is important to create an organizing committee with people who know how to have major amounts of fun.

For the junior-high and high-school level, you'll probably want to bring a hot Christian band, strange and wild video clips, tons of snacks and perhaps a couple of standup comedian acts. Be sure to put aside the religious expectations that often go with the season. These youth are wanting to go out and "find a good time." Unfortunately, that usually results in destructive behavior: excessive drug use, pregnancies, drunken driving, even deaths. It makes a lot of sense for a church to advertise to its community's adults that it wants to provide a safe environment for a total blast. This fits our Christian calling (protecting youth in their vulnerability) and makes for a clear witness.

Think through the different age groups, on up the ladder of years. If you have people with the energy to design different parties for various groups, go for it.

One large suburban church offered a very helpful service throughout the twenty-four hours of New Year's celebrations: a free taxi service. The members of the church visited several bars where parties were scheduled and offered business cards announcing the phone number for the free service. The bartenders were grateful for this kind of help. The church members explained that they would be staffing the church switchboard all night and would respond to requests not only for a ride home but also for a "drive" home for the person's car.

Many people in that suburb woke up at strange hours on January 1 to find a little card and a fruit basket inside their door. The note said, "We hope the hangover isn't too harsh! And we hope this will be a good year for you and your special friends." It was signed, "The folks of ABC Fellowship."

For many of the participating Christians, this was their first time darkening the door of a bar. Now they know a little of the threat some people feel as they climb the steps to the sanctuary door for the first time. (And who knows, maybe a few of their hungover friends will one day dare to do *that.)*

29
Thanksgiving

· · · · · · · · · · · ·

Two themes are traditionally a part of the Thanksgiving celebration. The first, and more common, has to do with the gratitude we feel for physical provision. This celebration is colorfully expressed in farming communities, where the tie to the land is immediate. Seed goes in and life sprouts forth from death. The bounty of the land is an extension of the bounty of God's hand.

This by itself is an entirely appropriate reason to celebrate Thanksgiving. But it's difficult in a society as affluent as ours to keep in mind that we are still dependent upon God for our daily living. Some of us slip into the erroneous idea that the fruit of the earth is the fruit of democratic capitalism. It's good for our spiritual health to do some serious reflection on the generosity of the Lord at least once a year.

But why not enlarge the celebration?

A second, less often articulated element of the Thanksgiving holiday is that it was initiated by aliens, strangers to the land who were not sure of their chances of survival. To be sure, many died of starvation and sickness in the early days, so for the survivors, Thanksgiving came from the heart.

Now, we need to recognize that some people say it's insensitive to observe a holiday that was linked to white Westerners' taking over Native American lands. We don't think that these criticisms should be taken lightly. The North American church still has some difficult and sensitive work ahead in thinking through the moral response to that history.

Nonetheless, the Bible clearly articulates our need to welcome the stranger and the alien. We think that Thanksgiving is a perfect time of year to focus on our nation's aliens and strangers.

We suggest that members of the church or fellowship who themselves were once aliens or strangers to this land should team up with a group of "pure-blooded" Americans from the same fellowship. Think through together how you can reach out to people who still feel unwelcome, unsettled or just plain uncomfortable. One of the clear hallmarks of Christians is that they don't discriminate against people because of the color of their skin, their national heritage or their religious affiliation. (We would *all* be in some deep hot water if Jesus related to us according to these kinds of prejudices!)

In fact, we think it makes sense to focus specifically on people our culture tends to denigrate: undocumented Hispanic workers, Arabs from Libya or Iraq—it's easy enough to come up with a list. Be sensitive and thoughtful: What would they enjoy? How can we best link into their needs? How can they enrich us?

Why not make this an opportunity for education? See if these people would like to attend a special Thanksgiving celebration at the church. Design the theme of the evening around their culture. Bring in their music, dances, clothes, food and other cultural items. Have them tell stories about their country and people, and ask them to relate the special difficulties they've had in adjusting to North American society.

The sensitivity of the church will be greatly enhanced through this encounter, and a group of people the government calls "aliens" will have experienced one of the most prized elements of the Christian faith.

30
Halloween

· · · · · · · · · · · ·

OOOOOOOOOooooo . . . Screeeeeeeeeeeeccchhh . . . Meooooowwww!

Goblins, witches, ghosts and Freddy.

Another good ol' American holiday: strange when you think about the meanings of the words "holy day" and "holy evening." As is always the case with our witness, we have the option of withdrawing from this national event—of becoming defensive and losing yet a little more ground, another opportunity to influence society. It need not be so.

Most of what goes on during Halloween is not much different

from what happens on Saturday morning cartoons or in a Walt Disney animated movie. Much of it is creative fun. To be sure, the dark side of the spirit world thrives, and demonic territory is not child's play. But Halloween as most people observe it is basically just another Hallmark opportunity. The celebration is a cultural fact, and people look forward to the fun and games associated with it.

Our suggestion is that your fellowship do just that—offer fun and games. What we have here is essentially another chance for people to rub shoulders with the church in a way that is not threatening. A medium-sized rural church in the Northwest has caught on to this idea and pretty much steals the show for the entire town on Halloween Eve. They call together the pastors of all the surrounding churches and offer the use of their church gymnasium for an all-town party. Local businesses join the effort. Different groups take responsibility for game booths, and the result is a virtual carnival. Prizes, refreshments and laughter flow. Practically all the youth in the town show up at some point in the evening. The point is made: church doesn't have to be irrelevant.

A more ambitious effort is creating a massive haunted house. Churches may tackle this project in conjunction with groups like Young Life and Youth for Christ.

We aren't excited about the excesses of some Christian groups' haunted houses—telling people that they will live a hell "just like this" for all eternity if they don't make a commitment to Jesus. One California group simulated the abortion of a fetus in one of the inside scream rooms and then asked, "Have you done this to anyone?" We're not sure that is the best way to convince folks how tragic abortion is.

Our witness should always respect the persons we hope to reach and never bombard them with an alternative agenda. If you promise a good evening of fun for Halloween, then deliver. At the same time, we do not think it's a bad idea to advertise your Christian identity up front. Flyers and posters that promote the haunted house could say, "We think it's a SCREAM to follow Jesus. Jesus takes the FRIGHT out of life. Come visit the best little haunted house in town." Or words to that effect.

31
Other Special Days
·············

We close this section of *50 Ways You Can Share Your Faith* simply by suggesting that there are many more calendar events waiting to be used creatively in our witness:

☐ Father's Day

☐ Mother's Day

☐ Grandparents' Day

☐ Martin Luther King, Jr., Day

☐ Wedding anniversaries

☐ How about your church or fellowship creating a *new* annual holiday? For example, Family Day, a time to celebrate the bonds of love between mother, father, child, husband, wife, brother, sister, grandparents . . .

In each case ask yourself: What unique and surprising angle can we, the people of God, bring to this celebration? We want to stress that you use your creativity to encourage, support and nurture people. Don't fall into the trap of using these celebrations to preach, condemn or "correct" people's lifestyles.

We hope you enjoy building the bridges of love!

III

Public Preaching

Up to this point in *50 Ways You Can Share Your Faith*, we have suggested how you can gently come alongside people in the name of Jesus. Here are six different ways you can get more direct and do some "preaching." Admittedly, these activities don't look a whole lot like traditional preaching, but the same principle is there: articulating to the public the claims of Jesus Christ. Some of these ideas call for an all-out "come up front and make your confession of faith," while others quietly leave the door ajar.

32
Live Rock
· · · · · · · · · · ·

Today's youth are continually bombarded with values and lifestyle choices that are antibiblical. Peer pressure to conform to those values is almost too intense for any young person to resist.

The church has not always been helpful in this regard. By creating unnecessary rules and taboos, we often push people away from the protection and support the church could provide. The message we regularly give youth is that not only must they reject many of their subgroup's values, but, in fact, they must reject their entire youth culture. Well, teenagers will almost always choose their culture over church.

One of the key elements of any culture is its music. It is criminal that many churches have tried to cut youth off from this aspect of their culture. Clearly, there *are* songs with despicable lyrics. That's not the issue. Rather than forbidding teenagers to listen to the bad stuff, you can help them by allowing some honest listening and discussion, as a knowledgeable youth pastor or other adult guides them into wisely evaluating what is harmful and what isn't.

Tremendous poetry and inspiring music are being written by today's youth—songs that deserve the praise of any honest critic. The church has the opportunity to make a bridge back to young people through music.

Our suggestion is simple. Get together with the talented young musicians in your fellowship (if you have chased them all away, be brave—take a step of faith and link up with a fellowship that attracts these youth). Think together of ways you can promote local contemporary Christian rock concerts.

We need to be clear here—we're not talking about the kind of music Mom and Dad like. We are talking about contemporary, loud, long-haired, leathered, *Christian* rock and roll. This music uses the language of young people—and the lyrics are solidly Christian.

If your fellowship has no experience with this kind of outreach, contact the editors of *Contemporary Christian Music* magazine. Explain your goal and ask for help in finding a promoter in your region who can handle all the logistics. There are dozens of people who do this for a living. They do the hard work, take the financial risks and walk away with the money. You get connected with someone who understands the business and a group that delivers the right sound. And you will succeed in building relationships with youth—relationships that may grow deeper over time.

33
Evangelism Event

· · · · · · · · · · · ·

There are certain events, national and international, that are natural environments for personal evangelism. An organization that has developed a reputation for this sort of evangelism is Youth With A Mission (YWAM). During the 1984 Olympics in Los Angeles, for example, YWAM coordinated an evangelistic program for tourists.

The leaders of the organization met with church staff from Los Angeles and surrounding towns. Together they planned a massive effort that recruited fourteen thousand youth to spend two weeks in evangelism. Churches opened their sanctuaries for sleeping bags and turned over their kitchens and buses. The call for volunteer evangelists brought people from across the United States and from dozens of nations around the world.

An intensive time of training prepared people to communicate the simple message of salvation. Others were trained in street mime, drama, music, storytelling and literature distribution. A special newspaper was created for the Olympics that covered the events but also spoke of Christianity. Phone numbers and addresses indicated where tourists and local residents could go for more information regarding Christ.

Here is a list of the outcomes:

☐ As many as eight thousand personal decisions for Christ were made.

☐ Perhaps as many as 100,000 heard the gospel in a fresh, unusual way.

☐ Fourteen thousand youth were trained to be creative in sharing their faith.

☐ These fourteen thousand youth went through an intensive discipleship course that involved prayer, worship and quiet times every day for three weeks.

☐ Nine hundred pastors got together to serve each other and the Lord of the harvest.

☐ A local organization continues to bring together these pastors for prayer and other coordinated events.

This is no small accomplishment! Now, the idea is a good one, but massive. Part of the genius of an organization like YWAM is its ability to pull together volunteers for temporary assignments. We think their idea is well worth imitating on a local level.

Begin to look at the calendar for similar opportunities. If you want some help, contact YWAM (address in the back under Organizations) and see whether they would join you for a cooperative outreach.

34
Crusade
· · · · · · · · · · ·

Billy Graham has occupied a place on the list of the world's ten most admired men for more than two decades now. His ministry is a curious phenomenon: no glitz or emotionalism, just a simple presentation of the claims of Christ and then the overwhelming response of an audience that apparently was waiting for this special moment to respond. Graham says that most of the work of evangelism has been done before these people show up at the crusade. Friendships and contact with the church have brought people to the brink of decision, and Graham simply serves as the final nudge.

We think it's a good idea to learn from the world's most renowned evangelist. Research expert George Barna tells us that half the people in church pews haven't yet made a personal decision to place their trust in Jesus. Our evangelistic task is closer to home than we realize.

Our suggestion is: Plan an annual evangelism week. Announce to the congregation that this special week will have two emphases.

The first will be church members in the pew. Be friendly and clear about the fact that many people in the church have been exploring the life of Christ but haven't yet taken that step of faith. This special week is designed with them in mind. They can think through their spiritual journey and consider whether this is the time to join the family of faith.

The second focus will be people we all know who seem to be close to the Christian life but are not a part of the church. They have thought a lot about Christianity but have not had the opportunity to get close to people who can help them think through their questions regarding life with Jesus.

The week-long program should, in our opinion, have at least the following elements:

☐ A private opportunity to declare an interest in Christ. This could be as simple as a card that is put in the offering plate to request a visit or phone call from a church member.

☐ A minicrusade that has an excellent program of music each evening and a simple gospel message explaining the way to personal salvation, culminating in an opportunity for public confession of faith on Sunday morning.

☐ A first-rate slate of Saturday seminars that address the concerns of people who are considering the Christian faith. And how about a special, nonthreatening workshop that allows people to ask all the questions they want without feeling they've been put on center stage? A simple mechanism for this would be to pass around a box for anonymous questions. All the cards would be read aloud and answered during the workshop.

If Barna is correct in his research, many churched people will find this to be their golden opportunity to begin following Jesus.

35
Debate

· · · · · · · · · · · ·

We have an idea that we think will work on the college campus. Quite often a particular issue springs up on a campus and becomes the defining intellectual or social concern for the entire semester. Student bodies are transitory enough in their thinking that these same issues disappear almost entirely by the next semester. That fact does not diminish how much impact the concern has.

These concerns present evangelistic opportunities for two reasons. First, by nature Christians are bothered about intellectual and social issues. They aren't simply bridges to evangelism—the integrity of the gospel requires our engagement. The second reason, which can only follow the first, is that public engagement offers a chance to point to the character and requirements of the Christian faith.

Gather a group of Christians who are interested in exploring these critical issues. Then pray together quite regularly to develop of spirit of love and humility. Too often Christians express their intellectual notions to the public with a haughty, better-than-thou attitude—one that clearly goes against the grain of the gospel. Ask the Lord to give you wisdom and guidance as you try to determine the best way to enter the public debate. Once you've selected your subject, it is time to do the hard work of planning, promotion and presentation.

Begin with the professors on campus. Does anyone there articulate the issue in a way that will encourage effective public debate? If not, approach local chapters of national student organizations such as Navigators or InterVarsity, and ask them for a resource person. You may want to contact the Christian College Coalition in Washington, D.C. The coalition is the nerve center for more than seventy Christian colleges and universities and would know of professors who have strong academic credentials and first-rate public speaking skills.

Once you have the program lined up, see if you can secure the cosponsorship of one or more academic departments—for example, philosophy or religion. If your guest lecturer carries the right credentials, you may easily get the department on board. Print up the flyers, and inform the school newspaper, community newspaper and local clergy fellowship.

At the event itself, be as professional and respectful as possible. Allow a significant time for interaction with the speaker afterward, and rather than being overtly evangelistic ("We hope all of you will discover the means to personal salvation with Christ"), invite people to continue the discussion with you ("This has been a cooperative presentation of the ABC, DEF and GHI campus Christian fellowships. We welcome your ongoing involvement and discussion with us on these relevant issues. Literature in the back of the room will orient you to our activities and programs").

36
New Church in Town

· · · · · · · · · · · ·

Not many churches make the decision to become
downwardly mobile. A large West Coast church was facing the
need to relocate. The wonderful problem of a growing congregation led to a decision-making process and the notion that God
wanted them to buck the national church-growth trend of moving further into the suburbs—and further into irrelevance.

They relocated into a multi-ethnic urban community.

As is true of any neighborhood, this community included
people who were curious about the gospel but had few "new
leads" toward an approachable church. As the church leaders

thought through their relocation strategy, they decided to throw a public party, welcoming themselves into the neighborhood and inviting others to join in the celebration.

A couple of weeks before the event, church members hit the sidewalks with flyers announcing the party in the park. The park is central to the community and is not considered a religious location. Attractions included face painting for kids, balloons, music, drama, free hot dogs and punch, Bibles and a short evangelistic sermon. The local D.A.R.E. unit and fire station were invited to put up booths to give information about drug abuse and fire hazards.

More than a thousand community members showed up for the event, twenty-five people made decisions right there in the park to follow Jesus, and as you might guess, a good number of others decided to give this new church a try on Sunday.

37
Protest
· · · · · · · · · · ·

Some people are born with more than their fair share of *chutzpah*. This idea is for them.

The Bible is clear that we should not separate the character of God from our public witness. Too often we feel comfortable just calling for a step of faith into Christ's forgiveness. But witness can be a much broader ministry.

In the Old Testament, the picture of a just God is predominant. God tells the Israelites that they must treat the alien and stranger lovingly, that they're to feed the hungry and care for the homeless. The outcome of this sort of lifestyle is not only that people are cared for directly (a sufficient goal by itself) but, in addition, that the light of God is able to shine through as a testimony to the character of Yahweh.

When Christians take a public stand against injustice, they are in fact pointing to the character of God.

Our suggestion, then, is that you round up some support if you feel a strong call to publicly address injustice in your town—whether it be harsh treatment of aliens, unfair zoning laws for the poor, inadequate medical care for infants or abortion of the unborn. Make sure that people are committed to praying with you and for you in this ministry.

Your method of protest must not work against your goal of pointing people to the character of God. In all your dealings, treat people with dignity and respect. If they choose not to respond in kind, that is their option. Do not become a smug abused protester. Seek help from your friends to remain a servant, both to God and to the people you are confronting, and allow each insult to spur your commitment to prayer.

If you become discouraged by the negative reactions you receive from those in power (the people against whom you are protesting), remember that you have offered great encouragement to those who are being hurt by the unjust practices. You have told these people some very good news: Jesus is a friend to the poor.

IV

Personal Giving

• • • • • • • • • • • • • •

There is no way we can really take on the whole world with the evangelistic message, so we might just as well give up on the idea, right? Wrong. We think it is reasonable for all of us to take inventory of our lifestyle and make simple, measured decisions about our time, money, "chance" encounters, vacations, prayer life and gift giving. It makes sense that we take little steps toward our heart's desire rather than giving up from a sense that there's too much to do.

38
Prayer

· · · · · · · · · · · ·

Prayer is good news to Christians for two reasons.
First, it is a form of ministry open to anyone who loves Jesus
and is looking for a place to become involved in kingdom work.
Second, it is effective. The Holy Spirit took care to leave us with
a record of the vital importance of prayer: Jesus was over-
whelmed by the pressing needs of the world, having just en-
countered every sort of physical, emotional and spiritual infir-
mity, and he said to his disciples, "Pray!"

Prayer, of course, has several functions. We focus here on two
evangelistic ideas. The first is personal. We suggest that you ask

God to make you sensitive to a few people who live outside the faith. Perhaps they will include family members, coworkers, next-door neighbors or heads of state. Make it your business to become acquainted with their lives, so that your prayers for them are directed toward actual needs.

Don't take on more of a commitment than is reasonable for your lifestyle. We think it makes sense to build up toward a vigorous prayer life rather than face depression from doing the reverse. We also recommend that you involve one other person in your prayer life—someone who has taken on a similar goal. You can encourage each other to be faithful in your commitment. We suggest you meet once a month or so to pray over each other's lists of friends.

The second suggestion we have is to join in a "concert of prayer." There is a growing movement in the United States that is a tremendous example of unity among believers as they bring to Jesus the needs of the nation and the world. The "concert of prayer" (COP) idea is several hundred years old but was recently reintroduced to the American public by David Bryant, founder and director of Concerts of Prayer International.

This is how it works: You join church leaders from your area in a commitment to hold a monthly prayer meeting that lasts about an hour and a half. An official concert of prayer is divided into three sections—worship, prayer for God to bring revival to our nation, and prayer for God to send laborers to regions of the world where his name is not yet known. Because the format is easily followed, interesting, fast-paced and focused, many people who do not usually join prayer meetings find this an exciting way to be involved.

Contact your pastor to see if the idea has already landed in your town. If not, contact Concerts of Prayer for a starter kit. The address is listed in the "Organizations" section of this book.

39
Time

. . . .

According to several prominent social theorists, the current measure of one's wealth is how much "free" time one has. The demands of earning a living and the tendency to extend our work hours so we can buy items we may not even want result in burnout, depression, heart attacks and broken relationships.

As people are pushing to simplify their lives, is it reasonable to expect them to gear up for evangelistic action? Probably not—unless the notion of time is considered.

Our suggestion is that you take inventory of your time. Ask how your present lifestyle meshes with your real priorities. Some people insist that how you spend your time is the actual measurement of your priorities, but we don't think it's that simple. We need help managing ourselves in a modern, fast-paced, demanding society.

Ask yourself, "Can I afford to budget ten minutes of my week to purposeful evangelism?" If the answer is yes, pick an idea in this book that takes ten minutes per week. There is no need to depress yourself by leaping into immense time commitments that you know can't last beyond the first couple of weeks. Neither does it make sense to become depressed through inaction. All of us can do *something* of value.

Once you are giving your ten minutes a week to evangelism, you can slowly increase it to the point where it fits your personal sense of priority or calling.

There is one other way to manage your time—setting aside large blocks of time once or twice a year. For example, you may want to give a week of your vacation to a special evangelistic effort in your community or overseas. If so, plan that into your calendar. It is not likely to materialize any other way.

40
Money
. . . .

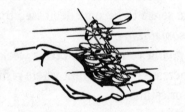

There just never seems to be enough money to meet personal needs. And when you add to that demand the overwhelming cries of a society in need—well, what's the average Christian to do?

Don't despair. That's our first piece of advice. It really does seem as if our little contribution to society is insignificant, but we must remember the parable of the mustard seed. The Lord was trying to show his disciples that though our efforts of faith might seem to produce no more than a little weed the size of a mustard plant, they in fact produce a tree so large even the birds alight there to build nests.

When we give funds toward evangelism, we are doing two things. First, we are making an offering to the Lord. And it is an offering that smells sweet to him. It doesn't matter what size altar we build, or how much we pour on top before lighting the offering—what we bring to the Lord with a sincere heart produces an aroma that is delightful to the King. Second, our offering has practical significance. It truly does help bring the gospel message to people who do not know Jesus personally.

We suggest that you begin your evangelism stewardship with a small step of faith. Decide how much you can realistically afford to give to evangelism without stressing your family budget beyond reason. Be faithful in giving that amount, and thoroughly enjoy the process. You may want to slowly increase the amount you give—perhaps you can add a couple more dollars to your total each month.

Stay away from the emergency appeals. They are usually carefully planned by large Christian corporations that have learned they can extract a lot more from the Christian public if they create the sense that "without your sacrificial help at this time, we just won't make it." The idea is that we'll feel honored to be so important to them—and guilty if we do not help them and thus cause their doom. So we give. What actually occurs is that we lose control of our giving and are suckered.

Think through the types of evangelistic efforts you'd like to support. We recommend that you put very little of your funds into the big building programs and TV ministries. These do not have a reputation for winning many to Jesus. Look first for the sort of ministry that involves direct contact with people. Relationships are the essence of evangelistic outreach. Perhaps there are some creative ideas in this book that you can invest in—outreach efforts that are not likely to win the average church dollar.

We also suggest that you find a friend who would be happy to enter into mutual accountability—someone who is also at the point of beginning to give regularly. Don't be shy in getting started—you will be encouraging someone else who is not likely to give without the partnership. Get together once a month over coffee or tea to share the news on how your money was spent. Enjoy the good feelings that rightly come from giving your "firstfruits."

41
Calendar Gifts

· · · · · · · · · · · ·

Buying gifts for family members and coworkers can be stressful. We don't want to give another plaque or toy the person doesn't really want. We're not that excited about giving another certificate to their favorite junk-food restaurant, nor do we think it's special to give a box of candy.

There are ways to link our gift-giving with our desire to bring people a little closer to Jesus: Give gifts that match their interests and fulfill our desire to create a bridge to Jesus. Here are some examples:

☐ If you are giving to a young child, how about a good set of cassettes that play mellow music with a solid Christian message? Cassettes with bedtime stories are also available. The best in the market is a series by the "Donut Man." His material is carried by Integrity Music. You might also look into the children's workshop music of the Vineyard Christian Fellowship or Maranatha! Music.

☐ For kids who are just a little bit older, you might consider a videocassette. "McGee and Me" videos enchant them. Talk to your local Christian bookstore manager for the latest from Focus on the Family/Tyndale House and other companies that are working to provide wholesome Christian entertainment.

☐ There is a great selection of books, magazines and contemporary music for teens. Again, consult your local Christian bookstore for the latest. Books range from historical and fantasy novels to contemporary discussions of sex and AIDS. Music runs the whole spectrum of sound, from heavy metal to country.

☐ For adults, our advice is basically the same. Get to know the interests of the person for whom you are buying and look for something appropriate. Don't limit yourself to the Christian book or music store. Secular releases by groups such as Ladysmith Black Mambazo are entirely appropriate for music lovers off the beaten track, and Annie Dillard's *Pilgrim at Tinker Creek* would make a great gift for any literature lover.

If you run out of ideas, brainstorm with others who have the same problem. It may not be realistic to give a gift this expensive to all your friends (prices can kill your budget), but it does make sense to focus on a few people and begin to feel that your gifts are bridging the gap to eternity.

42
Sovereign Encounters

· · · · · · · · · · · ·

There is an important understanding that goes with evangelism: God is actively involved in drawing people to himself. God is the ultimate evangelist, and in the final analysis, evangelism is God's responsibility. Our part of the deal is that we get the privilege of cooperating with God's activities in the world.

Sometimes the number of people who do not appear to have a personal relationship with Christ seems overwhelming—we freeze and do nothing. But we can take heart from the fact that God is already involved in touching the lives of those around us.

We are never alone in our evangelism attempts, nor are we in charge.

Our suggestion is simply that we take the risk of cooperating with God. Ask for a sovereign encounter. Trust God to bring into your life someone who is ready to hear the splendid news of salvation. God, in his way, will nudge you toward someone you may or may not know.

These sovereign encounters can be quite surprising. A family in Los Angeles decided to trust God to use them in evangelism. They were nervous about this concept of witnessing, so they prayed that God would bring someone right to their door. It took a lot of faith to say that prayer. Within that very week a family of four knocked on their front door and announced that they were looking for help to become Christians! Imagine the joy of leading a whole family into a relationship with Jesus—right in your own living room.

Some advice: Don't get too uptight as you meet people you think God may have brought your way. Relax with the knowledge that God knows your heart for evangelism and will never condemn you for acting out of this natural desire. Rest in God's character and take the plunge.

43
Travel
. . . .

Some of us, particularly high school and college students, teaching professionals and retired persons, have the option of taking extended trips to other parts of the nation or the world. The travel industry is well aware of this fact and offers targeted travel packages that bring in billions of dollars each year.

Well, why not combine your traveling itch with reaching out for Jesus?

Each year, as many as 200,000 North American Christians take anywhere from ten days to three months out of their normal routine to join their local church or a parachurch ministry in a short-term mission project. Such outreach ranges from evangelism to construction to teaching English. And the locations are as diverse as Beijing, Soweto and London.

Besides giving you the opportunity to see another part of the world, these trips allow you to contribute to the worldwide ministry of the church in a structure that is suited to your abilities and needs. And it is usually much cheaper than your typical tour package.

Here are a few examples of what has been done:

☐ A farming church in the Northwest linked up with a mission agency to construct a school for missionary kids in Guatemala.

☐ A group of students from a Christian college spent the summer in Soweto, teamed up with black South African Christians, learning what it means to pursue the difficult work of reconciliation in a nation governed by racism.

☐ Another group of college students spent their summer in the Commonwealth of Independent States teaching English at the Kiev Pedagogical Institute and sharing friendship with the students among whom they lived.

☐ An inner-city church sent its youth group to spend an entire summer helping in a rural ministry in Mississippi.

College students may also arrange to receive academic credit for time overseas.

If you live near a Christian college, see if you can link up with its programs. Also, check with local pastors to find out if they have any experience with doing these types of trips.

Two resources will be of particular help as you plan your ministry travel. The first, *The Short-Term Mission Handbook,* is

a complete guide to short-term missions. It will tell you every-
thing you want to know about setting up trips. The second,
Bridge Builders, is a consulting organization that specializes in
arranging all the details of short-term projects. Both are listed
at the back of this book.

V

Personal Growth and Resources

● ● ● ● ● ● ● ● ● ● ● ● ● ●

Evangelism is a lifelong journey. Each of us is a witness in some fashion. But most of us would like to grow in our ability to reach out to others.

That's what this section is all about. It is by no means a complete listing of the materials and ideas available for you to use, but it's a beginning point. We trust you will be encouraged by these materials to find practical ways to live out your desire to be a servant of Jesus' love.

44

Push the Boundaries

· · · · · · · · · · · · ·

It's easy to be a full-time Christian. By that we mean someone who is always involved in religious activity, meeting in religious buildings, mixing with religious people . . . you get the picture. Perhaps one of the reasons we need so many seminars, resources and schemes to help us evangelize is that we are completely out of touch with people who do not make the church their primary center of activity—they are like foreigners to us.

We need to push the boundaries—expand our circle of influence so that we are naturally around people who don't know

Jesus. "The world" will become less of a mystery to us, and we will find it much easier to enter conversations about our faith. Here are some of the ways we recommend for pushing out those walls:

☐ Go to the movies regularly. Choose the films that seem to be receiving the most notice in the press; these are likely to impact people's opinions and actions. Look for those that are trying to say something about society—you can usually expect that kind of treat from Woody Allen or Steve Martin, for example.

☐ In a similar fashion, look for books that are making the best-seller lists. This is something we have to learn as we do, because there are *good* novels, political/social commentaries and psychological self-helps—and there are losers. You need to be willing to spend the time to learn how to tell which are the good books. They will help you understand people's feelings and attitudes.

☐ Join societies that discuss the arts. These groups are usually at the cutting edge of social debate. If you have not been around this sort of folks before . . . fasten your seat belt!

☐ Subscribe to newsletters and magazines that give you insight into people who do not think like you. (Or read them for free at your local library.) A typical conservative Christian would benefit from reading the *Utne Reader*, *Ms.*, *The Progressive* and *Greenpeace*. A typical liberal Christian would benefit from reading *National Review*, *American Heritage* and *U.S. News and World Report*.

☐ Watch TV programs that are impacting society. We don't mean you should become a TV addict, but you should be current enough to speak knowledgeably with others about the content of these shows.

□ Attend places or events that attract people unfamiliar to you. Examples could be the rodeo, the local bar or that church you always thought of as off the orthodoxy scale.

These stretching exercises can make us uncomfortable. We are putting ourselves in environments where we do not know the rules, environments we have been trained to avoid. These are all necessary encounters if we are to go into the world and build bridges of friendship to others who may be outside the faith. Too often we turn people away from Jesus simply because our limited exposure to others has allowed our prejudices (even racism and sexism) to grow. Christians should always be in the forefront of trying to understand others.

It is our opinion that if we take the risky step of expanding our boundaries, we'll discover that we have taken the chief evangelistic step—the step that educates *us* and makes us better prepared to carry out the evangelistic mandate. It is the most significant step we can take, and yet the one least encouraged by the church.

45
Watch the
Language
. . . .

The more we enter into other people's worlds, the more
we realize that we need to adjust our language. Many of us, in
our youth, did not blush at telling jokes about Poles, Jews,
African Americans, whites or dizzy blondes. Then we grew up a
little. As our world expanded, we realized we were belittling real
people. The humor leaves the joke at that point. People who
continue with racist or sexist language are telling us something
about their level of personal growth.

There is a need for growth in our evangelistic language that
is much easier to describe than to correct. As we have worked

to expand our own boundaries, we have come to discover that words such as "the unsaved," "non-Christian" and "unbeliever" feel like derogatory terms to those on whom we pin them. They are akin to "heathen," "nigger" or "faggot." These are negative and loaded images.

So what is the solution? Do we use terms like "seeker," "un-committed," "not yet a believer"? Frankly, we are not quite sure. But we do think that we should be sensitive enough to grow in this regard. Those of us who know Jesus personally choose to be identified positively and fully as Christian—we want the as-sociation. But we need not label people who do not follow the path we've chosen with a term that implies they are somehow *less* than we are.

We can agree to hold each other accountable in our use of language regarding race, ethnicity, gender, sexuality, religion. The more we remind each other of the way our terms offend, the more actively we will seek to build bridges that lead to friendship and better understanding of others.

46
Memorize
Scripture

· · · · · · · · · · · ·

There's not a whole lot we need to say about the evan-gelistic value of memorizing Scripture—the purpose is so obvious! But we want to emphasize this idea just in case it has gotten lost in the mix of all the other "contemporary" suggestions we've given.

The Bible gives us many reasons to "hide God's Word in our hearts." It keeps us from sinning, encourages us, provides wisdom in sticky moments and gives us the ability to testify "in season or out of season" to the person of Jesus Christ.

If memorizing Scripture has not been a part of your regular

discipleship program, we strongly encourage you to make your first leap. Don't go after it in chunks that are too large— you'll just depress yourself within a month. We recommend that you link up with a friend who has the same motivation. Together, select a couple or more verses you can memorize each week. Select verses that you think will help you in your desire to do evangelism.

If you are having trouble locating good verses, ask your pastor or fellowship leader. We would also suggest that you contact Navigators. This organization has developed memory systems that have helped thousands of Christians to store the Word in their hearts. Its address is listed in the "Organizations" section of this book.

We have two cautions to offer. First, stay away from the older translations. They may sound more "holy" in certain church circles, but in fact they reinforce the stereotype that Christianity belongs to a bygone era. Use a version you and your friends can easily understand.

And second, don't see your newly memorized Scripture as "ammunition" to fire at the enemy. These verses are memorized to help you recall specific truths so that you can *help* someone understand your love for Jesus. You may find you are summarizing or paraphrasing the passage as you talk with a friend, rather than reciting it and giving the reference. Tailor your presentation to your friend's need and readiness to hear. Still, memorizing is the surest way to have the right words to share!

47
Books
. . . .

This is not a complete list of books on evangelism, but it's a good start. Of course, you should always be on the lookout for new releases that will help you in your commitment to evangelism.

And as we mentioned earlier, look for novels and secular releases that provide a social commentary. If you have a particular interest in evangelism among certain groups of people—for example, Muslims—look for books that help you understand their culture, history and beliefs. Your local library, university, Christian college or religious center can help you locate those resources.

1. *Basic Christianity,* by John R. W. Stott (Downers Grove, Ill.: InterVarsity Press, 1958). A good tool for people who want to understand your basic beliefs.

2. *The Screwtape Letters,* by C. S. Lewis. This classic approaches the sticky question of heaven and hell, Christian living, and the devil's attempts to thwart God's plans.

3. *Out of the Saltshaker,* by Rebecca Manley Pippert (Downers Grove, Ill.: InterVarsity Press, 1979). This is a modern classic—by far the best-selling book on how to witness. Pippert offers a very human and encouraging view of evangelism.

4. *Reinventing Evangelism,* by Don Posterski (Downers Grove, Ill.: InterVarsity Press, 1989). Posterski calls for a fresh commitment to evangelism while offering insights into the barriers to effective witness in today's world.

5. *What Americans Believe,* by George Barna (Ventura, Calif.: Regal Books, 1991). An annual survey of values and religious views in the United States.

6. *The Frog in the Kettle,* by George Barna (Ventura, Calif.: Regal Books, 1990). This is a look at what Christians need to know about contemporary society if they are going to be serious in their evangelism. A highly practical, easy-to-read piece.

7. *The Short-Term Mission Handbook* (Evanston, Ill.: Berry Publishing, 1992). This is the complete guide to short-term missions, with contributions from more than sixty authors. Order from Berry Publishing, 701 Main St., Evanston, Ill. 60202.

8. *Vacations with a Purpose,* by Chris Eaton and Kim Hurst (Colorado Springs, Colo.: NavPress, 1991). A super-practical look at how you can organize your own short-term mission trip. A leader's guide is available from the same publisher.

9. *The Complete Student Missions Handbook,* by Ridge Burns and Noel Becchetti (Grand Rapids, Mich.: Zondervan, 1991). If you are working with high school or junior high students, this is the perfect tool for planning your short-term trips.

48

*Videos
and Movies*

· · · · · · · · · · ·

We suggest that you constantly monitor the movie scene to discover what is making a splash in the culture. These movies will bring you much closer to the people you hope to reach with Jesus' love. As we mentioned earlier, Woody Allen and Steve Martin are usually a good bet.

Here are some secular releases that we think are worth your time. You can pick them up at your local video store. (We are aware that some Christians have made the decision not to see any movies with an "R" rating. We respect that decision and do not have any interest in attempting to dissuade people from those personal moral choices. Unfortunately, most of the movies that teach us about our culture receive an "R" rating.)

1. *My Left Foot.* A sobering and compassionate look at the struggles of a severely handicapped person. Based on a true story.

2. *Mississippi Burning.* Insights into the social problems in the South during the 1960s. Based on an actual event.

3. *Cry Freedom.* A not-so-pretty picture of the struggle for justice in the Republic of South Africa. Based on actual events.

4. *Do the Right Thing.* An African-American portrayal of life.

5. *Children of a Lesser God.* Insights into the struggles of the hearing-impaired.

6. *The Mission.* Helps explain the history of religious and political abuse of South American Indians at the hands of the Spanish and Portuguese. Based on actual events.

7. *Dances with Wolves.* The Kevin Costner portrayal of Native American life.

The following videos have been produced by Christians to help us in our evangelism.

1. *The City for God's Sake.* A set of three videos narrated by urban specialist Ray Bakke. Order from MARC/World Vision International in Monrovia, California (818/303-8811).

2. *Cry Justice.* A twenty-five-minute video narrated by inner-city activist John Perkins. Order from the John M. Perkins Foundation, 1581 Navarro, Pasadena, CA 91103.

3. *The Search.* An exploration of the New Age movement. Order from 2100 Productions, Madison, Wisconsin (800/828-2100).

49
Newsletters and Magazines

· · · · · · · · · · · ·

If money is a problem, be sure to see whether your local library carries the journals we list below. If it doesn't, you may be able to convince the librarian to purchase subscriptions.

We have listed just Christian publications here. We've already suggested that you make a habit of reading secular publications that will expand your world view and your understanding of others. Spend as much time with the secular magazines as you do with the Christian publications listed below.

1. *Ministry Currents: Perspectives on Ministry in an Era of Change.* Published by the Barna Research Group, this quarterly

is the best there is if you want to stay current in ministry. $20.00 per year. Write to 722 West Broadway, Glendale, CA 91204.

2. *Context: Research to Make Religion Relevant.* Published by World Vision Canada; the best Canadian parallel to *Ministry Currents.* Quarterly and free. 6630 Turner Valley Rd., Missisauga, Ont. L5N 2S4, Canada.

3. *Together: A Quarterly Journal of World Vision International.* The best insights into the varied international attempts to bring together evangelism and community development. $15.00 per year. 919 West Huntington Dr., Monrovia, CA 91016.

50
Organizations
. . . .

There are so many good organizations that could as-sist you in your commitment to grow in evangelism. We've selected a few for you. We encourage you to take advantage of the many groups out there that will be willing to put you on their mailing list for free.

Navigators
P.O. Box 6000
Colorado Springs, CO 80934

InterVarsity Christian Fellowship
P.O. Box 7895
Madison, WI 53707

Campus Crusade for Christ
100 Sunport Lane
Orlando, FL 32809

Christian College Coalition
14 Fourth St. N.E.
Washington, DC 20002

Jews for Jesus
60 Haight St.
San Francisco, CA 94102

Concerts of Prayer
P.O. Box 36008
Minneapolis, MN 55435

Discover the World
3255 East Orange Grove Blvd.
Pasadena, CA 91107

Bridge Builders
9925 Seventh Way N., #102
St. Petersburg, FL 33702

Youth With A Mission
P.O. Box 406
Mountain Center, CA 92561